TOUCHSTONE

WORKBOOK 3B

MICHAEL MCCARTHY

JEANNE MCCARTEN

HELEN SANDIFORD

CAMBRIDGE
UNIVERSITY PRESS

CAMBRIDGE
UNIVERSITY PRESS

University Printing House, Cambridge CB2 8BS, United Kingdom

One Liberty Plaza, 20th Floor, New York, NY 10006, USA

477 Williamstown Road, Port Melbourne, VIC 3207, Australia

314–321, 3rd Floor, Plot 3, Splendor Forum, Jasola District Centre, New Delhi – 110025, India

79 Anson Road, #06–04/06, Singapore 079906

Cambridge University Press is part of the University of Cambridge.

It furthers the University's mission by disseminating knowledge in the pursuit of education, learning, and research at the highest international levels of excellence.

www.cambridge.org
Information on this title: www.cambridge.org/9781107651470

First published 2005
Second Edition 2014
20 19 18 17 16 15 14 13 12 11 10 9 8 7 6 5

Printed in the United Kingdom by Latimer Trend

A catalog record for this publication is available from the British Library.

ISBN 978-1-107-66583-5 Student's Book
ISBN 978-1-107-62875-5 Student's Book A
ISBN 978-1-107-69446-0 Student's Book B
ISBN 978-1-107-64271-3 Workbook
ISBN 978-1-107-62082-7 Workbook A
ISBN 978-1-107-65147-0 Workbook B
ISBN 978-1-107-62794-9 Full Contact
ISBN 978-1-107-63739-9 Full Contact A
ISBN 978-1-107-63903-4 Full Contact B
ISBN 978-1-107-68094-4 Teacher's Edition with Assessment Audio CD/CD-ROM
ISBN 978-1-107-63179-3 Class Audio CDs (4)

Additional resources for this publication at www.cambridge.org/touchstone2

Contents

Lesson **A** / Circle of friends

1 He's the guy . . .

Grammar | Choose the correct relative pronoun to complete each sentence. If a relative pronoun is not needed, circle the dash (—).

1. This is Andrew. He's the guy **which** /⊖ I met on vacation in Florida.

2. This is the dog **that / who** followed me on the beach one day. It turned out to be Andrew's dog. So I guess it was the dog **that / —** introduced us.

3. This is the amusement park **who / —** we went to on our first date. And this is the ticket for the first movie **that / who** we saw.

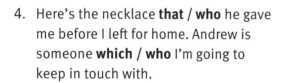

SUNSHINE CINEMA
SUMMER FUN
7:45 p.m.   Theater 8

4. Here's the necklace **that / who** he gave me before I left for home. Andrew is someone **which / who** I'm going to keep in touch with.

5. This is the letter **that / —** came three days after I got back. Inside is the photo **who / —** he took of me the day I left.

6. We talk every day. And this is the phone bill **who / that** I got yesterday!

cellular telecom   Phone Bill
EVA RODRIGUEZ

TOTAL DUE
$476.38

50

2 She's the girl . . .

Grammar | Complete the email with *who*, *that*, or *which*. Put the word in parentheses ( ) if the sentence is also complete without the relative pronoun. Sometimes more than one answer is possible.

> **New Message**
>
> To: mel_bes@cup.com
> From: camilleS@cup.com
> Subject: Estella and Ramiro
>
> Dear Melania,
>
> I'm so excited about some news _(that / which)_ I just got from a friend. You know Estella, right? She's my friend from Peru _____ I met in college. Well, last year I introduced her to that cute guy, Ramiro, _____ I used to work with. He had the desk _____ was across from mine. Anyway, a group of us used to go out together sometimes after work. One day, I invited Estella along. (I knew Ramiro was exactly the kind of guy _____ she would like.) We went to the Caribbean restaurant _____ I love on Essex Street. To make a long story short, they met that night, and now they're getting married. I just got the invitation. I can't wait for the wedding!
>
> Camille

3 I have a friend . . .

Grammar | Use the sentences in the box and *who*, *that*, or *which* to complete the sentences below. Put the relative pronoun in parentheses ( ) if the sentence is also complete without it. Sometimes more than one answer is possible.

Her family owns a store.	It served traditional Korean food.	The paper has rose petals in it.
I spoke to her in Korean.	✓She lives in South Korea.	The shop sells handmade paper.

1. I have a friend, Seung-Li, _who / that lives in South Korea_____ .
2. I met her in Seoul at the store _____ .
3. It is a very special shop _____ .
4. I bought some paper _____ .
5. She was the only person _____ .
6. Later, she invited me to a restaurant _____ .

4 About you

Grammar | Complete the sentences with true information. Use relative pronouns where necessary.

1. I have a friend _who speaks three languages_____ .
2. My neighbor is someone _____ .
3. I like stores _____ .
4. I take a class _____ .
5. I don't like the food _____ .
6. I know someone _____ .

1 Which particle?

Grammar and vocabulary **Circle the correct particle to complete each sentence.**

1. My sister's not home. She went **up /(away)/ along** for the weekend.
2. I grew **out / down / up** in Morocco, but now I live in California.
3. My brother isn't ready to settle **out / up / down**. He doesn't want to get married yet.
4. My mother's away on business now, but she plans to fly **away / along / back** next Tuesday.
5. I thought I had a doctor's appointment today, but it turns **out / up / down** that it's next week.
6. My best friend is moving **up / away / along** next month. I'm going to miss her.
7. I forgot to sign **back / out / up** for the class trip to the museum, so I can't go.
8. I sent my cousin an email last week, but he never wrote **back / away / out**.

2 Figure it out!

Grammar and vocabulary **Complete the sentences with the phrasal verbs in the box. Then complete the puzzle and the sentence below.**

come back	go away	sign up	✓write back
get along	grow up	work out	

1. When a friend sends you an email, you should _write back_ immediately.
2. If a relationship doesn't _____ , don't worry about it. It may be for the best.
3. If you want to _____ well with someone, be a good friend!
4. It's good to take a break from your usual routine and _____ for a few days.
5. It's fun to go on vacation, but it's always good to _____ home, too!
6. A lot of kids _____ in blended families these days.
7. One way to meet new people is to _____ for a class.

1. _w_ _r_ _i_ _t_ _e_ | b | _a_ _c_ _k_
2. ___ ___ | | ___ ___ ___ ___ ___
3. ___ | | ___ ___ ___ ___ ___ ___ ___
4. ___ ___ | | ___ ___
5. ___ ___ ___ ___ ___ | | ___ ___ ___
6. ___ ___ ___ ___ | | ___
7. ___ ___ ___ ___ | | ___

Some couples like to _____ _____ because they think it's fun to make up and get back together!

3 Breaking up is hard to do.

Grammar and vocabulary | Complete the conversation with the correct form of the phrasal verbs in the box. **Sometimes more than one answer is possible.**

✓break up	go out	turn out
get along	hang out	work out

Tina Hi, Jorge. You don't look so good. What's wrong?

Jorge Well, my girlfriend and I _broke up_ last week.

Tina Oh, no. You did? That's too bad. How long were you _____ with her?

Jorge About three months. I can't believe things didn't _____ . I mean, we _____ really well. I thought everything was fine.

Tina Yeah, you guys were always _____ together.

Jorge I know. We saw each other almost every day!

Tina Well, maybe that was the problem. Maybe she didn't want to spend every minute of every day with you.

Jorge Yeah, I guess you're right. Things didn't _____ the way I thought.

Tina Why don't you talk to her? Ask her what she wants in a relationship.

4 About you

 Grammar and vocabulary | **Answer the questions with true information.**

1. Who do you get along well with? Why?

    I get along well with my sister because we are very similar.

2. Do you like to go away for summer vacation?

    _____

3. Where do you and your friends like to hang out?

    _____

4. Do you always write back immediately when someone sends you an email?

    _____

5. Are there any classes you would like to sign up for?

    _____

6. Do you think you'll ever move far away from home?

    _____

1 I guess . . .

Rewrite each sentence with the two "softening" expressions in parentheses to complete the conversations.

1. A What's wrong with Jamil? He just yelled at me for turning on the TV.

   B *He's probably just tired.* He stayed
      <u>He's tired. (probably / just)</u>

      up all night. He had to finish a paper for school.

   A He always waits until the last minute to do his work.

   B I know. _____
      <u>He's disorganized. (I guess / kind of)</u>

   A Yeah, and he has so many activities at school.

      _____
      <u>He's doing too much. (I think / a bit)</u>

   B But it's good to be involved with your school.

   A That's true. _____
      <u>He's stressed out. (I guess / sort of)</u>

2. A Have you met Alissa yet? She's the new student in our class.

   B Yeah. I talked to her yesterday, but she didn't say much.

   A _____
      <u>She's shy. (maybe / just)</u>

   B Yeah, I'm sure she'll meet people soon.

      _____
      <u>It takes time. (just / a little)</u>

   A It's difficult when you don't know anyone.

   B I know. _____
      <u>It's hard to fit in. (I think / sort of)</u>

   A Yeah. _____
      <u>Making friends is hard. (I guess / in a way)</u>

2 It's spicy, though.

Conversation strategies Complete the conversations with the responses in the box.
Add *though* if appropriate.

> He's pretty shy.
> He's here for two weeks.
> ✓ I love Thai food.
>
> I'll find out when he's free.
> It was a little spicy.
> It was really nice.

1.   Lee   How was your dinner date last night?

    Kyra   Great. We went to a Thai restaurant that Wayne knows.

    Lee   Cool. *I love Thai food.*_____ What did you have?

    Kyra   Green curry with chicken and a vegetable dish.

    Lee   Was it good?

    Kyra   Yeah, the food was excellent. _____

            I don't usually like spicy food, but I really enjoyed it.

    Lee   Was it expensive?

    Kyra   Well, it was a little expensive. _____

2.   Becky   Brad, who's the new guy in your department?

    Brad   Oh, that's Bart. He's just visiting from the Los Angeles
         office. _____

    Becky   Only two weeks? That's too bad. He seems interesting.

    Brad   Yeah. _____ He's probably kind of lonely.

    Becky   Well, maybe we should invite him to dinner. Then we
         could show him around a little before he leaves.

    Brad   That sounds like a great idea. _____

3 About you

Conversation strategies Use true information to answer each set of questions. Respond to the
first question using "softening" comments. Then respond to the second
question using *though*.

1.   What's something you're bad at? What's something you're good at?
   I guess I'm kind of bad at playing tennis. I'm really great at playing chess, though.

2.   What's your worst quality? What's your best quality?
   _____

3.   What's difficult about learning English? What do you like about learning English?
   _____

4.   What annoying habit does one of your friends have? What's nice about him or her?
   _____

5.   What's your least favorite kind of music? What's your favorite kind?
   _____

1 Interactive communities

Reading **A** Read the article. What topics are discussed? Check (✓) all that apply.

☐ dating sites ☐ meeting people offline ☐ phone apps ☐ social networking

Using the online world to go offline

With our ability to connect to almost anyone in the world at any time, are we feeling more alone than ever? That's the question that critics of technology are asking. Some research suggests that people who use the Internet and social networks a lot often feel isolated and lonelier than people who don't. Supporters of online socializing disagree and point out that it's up to the user whether or not an online relationship becomes a meaningful, face-to-face one. After all, social networks, Internet companies, and app developers are merely doing their job – connecting users online. The next steps from online to offline are for us, the users, to take.

In fact, social networking websites often give us all the tools we need to move easily from an online relationship to an offline one. For example, there are websites that organize groups around particular interests. Perhaps you've just moved to a new city and want to meet people who have the same interests as you. You can sign up on websites that help you find others who enjoy the same hobbies. Many of these groups

plan face-to-face activities. It's a great way to connect with people you would never meet otherwise. There's no guarantee that you'll get along, but at least you'll have something in common.

Apps for cell phones or tablets can also help us connect with people offline in several ways. Some apps let you find friends nearby, find out what they are doing, and who's available to hang out. Other apps help you plan activities. You can send an invitation to friends electronically and include details about the activity, maps, and directions for how to get there. The people you invite can respond in the same way. There are also apps that recommend where you can meet people, for example, at restaurants or museums.

Technology doesn't have to isolate us. There are plenty of websites and phone apps that help us create social networks, both online and in real life. The trick is to make the effort. At some point, we have to pull our attention away from the screen in order to actually meet someone.

B Read the article again. Are the sentences true, false, or is the information not given? Write *T* (true), *F* (false), or *D* (doesn't say).

1. People who spend too much time online can feel lonely. _*T*_
2. The writer suggests that social networks are to blame for people's loneliness. ____
3. Websites that are for people with similar interests connect people that get along. ____
4. If you sign up for a website that organizes face-to-face activities, you'll meet new people that you like. ____
5. Most people only want to use websites and apps to find dates, not to find friends. ____
6. Technology can improve your relationships with your circle of friends. ____

2 Common ground

Writing | **A** Read the email. Then complete the sentences with *both*, *both of us*, or *neither of us*.

> **New Message**
>
> To: mitch_88@cup.com
> From: PhilJ@cup.com
> Subject: Your high school friend
>
> Dear Mitch,
>
> Remember me from high school? I'm the guy who sat behind you in world literature class. I got your email address from Kurt, the guy we ___both___ used to hang out with at lunchtime.
>
> I'll always remember that class. _____ hated reading those short stories, but we had to take the class for some reason. And _____ liked our teacher, Mr. What's-his-name. He wasn't a very good teacher at all. It's amazing that we _____ passed the final exam. Good thing we _____ stayed up late studying the night before.
>
> Anyway, I was talking to Kurt last week, and _____ would like to see you again. Maybe we can all meet and go out for dinner or something one day soon.
>
> Take care,
> Phil

B Write an email to an old friend you haven't seen in a long time. Include things you did and didn't have in common.

> **New Message**
>
> To: buddy1@cup.com
> From: buddy2@cup.com
> Subject: Long time no see!
>
> _____
> _____
> _____
> _____
> _____

Unit 7 Progress chart

What can you do? Mark the boxes. ☑ = I can . . . ？ = I need to review how to . . .	To review, go back to these pages in the Student's Book.
Grammar · ☐ write sentences with subject and object relative clauses.	66 and 67
☐ use phrasal verbs like *grow up*, *get along*, and *break up*.	68 and 69
Vocabulary · ☐ use at least 12 phrasal verbs.	68 and 69
Conversation strategies · ☐ use at least 6 expressions to soften comments.	70
☐ give a contrasting idea using *though*.	71
Writing · ☐ use *both*, *both of us*, and *neither of us*.	73

What if?

Lesson A / Wishes

 When you wish . . .

Grammar | **A** What are these people wishing for right now? Complete the sentences.

1. James _wishes he had a new car_ .

2. Emi and Sue _____ .

3. Joey _____ .

4. Esteban and Pilar _____ .

5. Al _____ .

6. Li-ming _____ .

B Complete the sentences about the people in part A.

1. If James ___had___ (have) more money, he ___would buy___ (buy) a new car.

2. If Emi and Sue _____ (live) in a bigger apartment, they _____ (have) more space.

3. If Joey _____ (be) taller, he _____ (score) more points.

4. If Esteban and Pilar _____ (have) two TVs, they _____ (not have) to watch the same TV shows.

5. If Al _____ (not be) a bad cook, he _____ (eat) better.

6. If Li-ming _____ (live) in the country, she _____ (be) much happier.

2 About you

Grammar | Write true sentences about your wishes.

My Wish List

1. I wish I _had more free time during the week_____ . (have)
   If I _had more free time during the week, I'd exercise more_____ . (have)

2. I wish I _____ . (be)
   If I _____ . (be)

3. I wish I _____ . (can)
   If I _____ . (can)

4. I wish I _____ . (not be)
   If I _____ . (not be)

5. I wish my parents _____ . (not be)
   If they _____ . (not be)

6. I wish my friend _____ . (be)
   If he or she _____ . (be)

7. I wish I _____ . (have)
   If I _____ . (have)

8. I wish I _____ . (not have to)
   If I _____ . (not have to)

9. I wish I _____ . (live)
   If I _____ . (live)

1 If I had a problem, . . .

Vocabulary | Circle the correct word to complete each sentence. Then decide if each sentence is true or false for you. Write *T* (true) or *F* (false). Correct the false statements.

1. __F__ If I had a problem, I would talk **for** / (**to**) / **about** my best friend.
   If I had a problem, I would talk to my Aunt Lisa.

2. _____ I always apologize **about** / **to** / **for** my mistakes.
   _____

3. _____ My friends never thank me **for** / **about** / **with** helping them.
   _____

4. _____ I always worry **for** / **about** / **from** taking tests!
   _____

5. _____ I often share books **to** / **with** / **about** my neighbors.
   _____

6. _____ If I forgot **with** / **from** / **about** a friend's birthday, I would feel bad.
   _____

2 Remind me about it.

Vocabulary | Complete the conversations with the words in the box.

ask for	✓ forget about	remind about	worry about
borrow from	lend to	talk to	
buy for	pay for	think about	

1. A Where's Marissa? I hope she didn't __forget__ __about__ our party.
   B I know. Let's call her and _____ her _____ it.

2. A Oh, no. I forgot my wallet. Can I _____ some money _____ you for lunch?
   B Oh, don't _____ _____ it. I'll get lunch. It's my treat!

3. A Do you think I should _____ this camera _____ my sister's birthday?
   B Why don't you _____ _____ her about it first?

4. A Can you _____ ten dollars _____ Lenny to buy a movie ticket?
   B I'm sorry. I can't. I have just enough to _____ _____ my own ticket.

5. A I think we're lost. Should we _____ someone _____ directions to the museum?
   B Not yet. I'm sure if I _____ _____ it for a minute, I'll remember how to get there.

3 Would you ask for an autograph?

Grammar | Complete the questions with the correct form of the verbs.

1. What _would you say_ (say) if you ___met___ (meet) a famous athlete?
   Would you ask (ask) for an autograph?

2. If you _____ (see) an accident, what _____ (do)?
   _____ (call) for an ambulance?

3. What _____ (do) if you _____ (have) a large spider
   on your leg? _____ (scream)?

4. If you _____ (break) your best friend's camera, how
   _____ (feel)? _____ (offer) to replace it?

5. How _____ (react) if your best friend _____ (win)
   a trip to Hawai'i? _____ (feel) jealous?

6. What _____ (say) to your neighbors if they
   _____ (complain) about your music? _____ (apologize)?

4 About you

Grammar | Answer the questions in Exercise 3. Write true information.

1. _If I met a famous athlete, I'd say, "I really admire you!"_
   I would definitely ask for an autograph.
   _____

2. _____
   _____
   _____

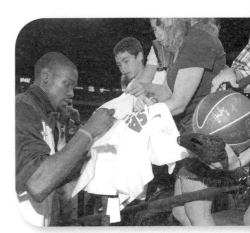

3. _____
   _____
   _____

4. _____
   _____
   _____

5. _____
   _____
   _____

6. _____
   _____
   _____

Lesson C **If I were you, . . .**

1 I'd choose . . .

Conversation strategies | Complete the conversation with the expressions in the box. Sometimes more than one answer is possible.

✓ if I were you, I'd	I would	I wouldn't	you could	you might want to

Serge I really want to take a vacation this summer, but I need to work, too.

Nina Well, _if I were you, I'd_ take a vacation first. You might not get another chance.

Serge Hmm. Maybe I should. Where's a good place to go – any ideas?

Nina Well, there are so many great places. I mean, _____ go anywhere. Have you been to Europe?

Serge No. I'd love to. It's kind of expensive, though.

Nina Well, _____ let that stop you! Seriously, you can always get a job there. There are programs for students who want to work abroad. _____ find out about them if I were you.

Serge I never thought of that.

Nina _____ look on the Internet and do a little research.

Serge Yeah. That's a great idea. So, I could work *and* take a vacation.

2 Good advice

Conversation strategies | Grace is having a bad day. Respond to her statements with advice.

1. **Grace** I didn't do very well on my math exam.
   You _If I were you, I'd talk to the teacher._

2. **Grace** Ouch! I just got a bad paper cut.
   You _____

3. **Grace** Oh, no! My car won't start.
   You _____

4. **Grace** I just stained my favorite sweater.
   You _____

62

3 You might want to . . .

Conversation
strategies | Look at the pictures. Complete the advice.

① You look tired. *I would get some* *coffee* .

② The sun's really strong. I _____
_____ .

③ It's very windy. If _____
_____ .

④ It's very cold. You _____
_____ .

4 That would be fun.

Conversation
strategies | Respond to each sentence with *That would be* and an appropriate adjective.

1. I'd really like to hike in the Himalayas.   *Wow. That would be awesome!*

2. Maybe we could go to the mall this afternoon.   _____

3. It would be great to win a million dollars.   _____

4. One day, I'm going to learn to tango.   _____

1 What do you regret?

Reading **A** Read the article about regrets. According to the article, which of the following factors affect how people regret things in life?

☐ age ☐ climate ☐ culture ☐ gender ☐ health ☐ income

Regrets? Too few to mention

Do you ever lie awake at night with regrets? Do you spend hours wishing you could change your life? __5__ If so, you're not alone. Regret – that negative feeling you have after a bad experience – is a fairly common human emotion. However, recent research suggests that while almost everyone experiences regret at some point or another, it is much more negative for some than for others.

What do we regret? According to research, we tend to regret decisions we made about our education, careers, romance, and parenting. We feel bad about things we did. ____ We wish we had different life opportunities, could make different choices, and relive moments with different outcomes. However, the nature and impact of regrets can vary across ages, sex, and cultures.

From the research, it would seem that the most striking difference in how regret affects people is between younger and older people. Younger people tend to regret the things they actually did, whereas older people regret the things they didn't do – their missed opportunities. Older people experience regret much more negatively. ____ Younger people are more likely to see a bad

experience as an important learning opportunity. They realize they made a mistake, and they use that to guide their decisions in the future. Older people don't feel they have the same chance to correct their actions and their outcomes.

Gender and culture can also affect what and how we regret. ____ According to some research, more women may regret lost romantic opportunities and family conflicts. More men may regret their decisions around career, money, and education. In cultures that put a high value on personal choice, such as the United States, people tend to have more regrets. In cultures where the family or the community makes more decisions, people have fewer regrets. Research suggests that the more choices we have, the more possibilities we have to regret.

So, if you find yourself staring at the ceiling at 3 a.m., what can you do to turn your regret into something positive? Use it to make better choices in the future. Realize that you couldn't control everything in the past situation. Take more chances in the future. ____ And be a little easier on yourself.

B Read the article again. Then add these missing sentences to the article by writing each number in the correct blank.

1. The differences between men and women are interesting.
2. We may feel worse about the things we didn't do.
3. Have more fun.
4. It can even lead to depression in some older people.
5. Do you torture yourself thinking about your mistakes?

C Choose the correct options to complete the sentences.

1. Feeling regret is **not common** / (**normal**).

2. The feeling of regret is **worse for some** / **the same for everyone**.

3. Older people mostly regret things they **did** / **didn't do**.

4. **Younger** / **Older** people feel they are in a better position to avoid the same mistakes.

5. Regret is **more** / **less** common when people make their own decisions.

6. The article suggests that in the end, regret is **useless** / **useful**.

2 If I won the lottery, . . .

Writing **A** Read the journal entry. Complete the sentences with the adverbs given and the correct verb forms.

> If I won the lottery, I ___'d definitely quit_____ (definitely / quit) my job, and
> I _____ (probably / not work) at all! If I were a millionaire,
> I _____ (definitely / buy) a house on the beach and one in the
> mountains. If I had two houses, I _____ (definitely / invite) my
> family and friends to visit, but I _____ (probably / not invite)
> them every weekend. I'd want some time for myself. If I had more time for myself, I'd
> write more, and I _____ (probably / try) to publish a book.
> What would the title of the book be? "How to Live Like a Millionaire," of course!

B Write a journal entry about what you would do if you were a millionaire. Use *definitely* and *probably* to show degrees of certainty.

> _____
> _____
> _____

Unit 8 Progress chart

What can you do? Mark the boxes. ✔ = I can . . .　　? = I need to review how to . . .		To review, go back to these pages in the Student's Book.
Grammar	☐ use *wish* + past form of verb for wishes about the present or future.	76 and 77
	☐ use *If* + past form of verb, followed by *would* / *could* + verb to talk about imaginary situations in the present or future.	76, 77, and 79
Vocabulary	☐ use the correct preposition after at least 12 verbs.	78
Conversation strategies	☐ give advice using expressions like *If I were you* and *You could*.	80
	☐ use *That would be* to comment on a possibility or a suggestion.	81
Writing	☐ use *definitely* and *probably* to show degrees of certainty.	83

Tech savvy?

Lesson A / Tech support

1 I have no idea why . . .

Grammar **A** Unscramble the questions.

1. which battery / Do you know / should / buy / I / ?
   Do you know which battery I should buy?

2. they / where / are / Can you tell me / ?
   _____

3. when / you / Can you remember / it / last changed / ?
   _____

4. it / Do you have any idea / how much / costs / ?
   _____

B Unscramble the statements.

1. why / isn't / I have no idea / working / it
   _____

2. last changed it / when / I don't know / I
   _____

3. two / I / if / I wonder / should / batteries / buy
   _____

C Complete the conversation with the questions and statements from parts A and B.

Woman   Excuse me. Can you help me?

Clerk   Sure. What seems to be the problem?

Woman   It's my camera. *I have no idea why it isn't working.*

Clerk   Hmm. Let me look at it. It might be the battery. _____

Woman   No, I can't. _____ I'm not sure if I've ever changed it.

Clerk   Well, you definitely need a new one.

Woman   _____

Clerk   You need a 3.7 volt battery.

Woman   _____

Clerk   They're $39.99 each.

Woman   Great. _____

Clerk   Sure. They're at the back of the store. Here, let me show you.

Woman   Thanks. _____ Maybe I should have an extra one.

Clerk   That might be a good idea.

2 I wonder . . .

Grammar | **A** Tara wants to download some music from the Internet. Rewrite the questions she wants to ask her friend Kwang.

1. Can you download songs from this website?
2. How do you put them on your phone?
3. Is there a charge for each song?
4. Can you buy just one song?
5. How do you pay for the songs?
6. How do you make a playlist?
7. Are there any free songs?
8. Can I put the songs on my tablet, too?

1. I wonder *if you can download songs from this website* _____ .
2. Can you tell me _____ ?
3. Do you know _____ ?
4. Do you have any idea _____ ?
5. Do you know _____ ?
6. Can you remember _____ ?
7. I wonder _____ .
8. Do you know _____ ?

B Kwang doesn't know the answers to Tara's questions. Write his replies using the expressions in the box. Use each expression twice.

I don't know	I can't remember	I have no idea	I'm not sure

1. *I don't know if you can download songs from this website.* _____
2. _____
3. _____
4. _____
5. _____
6. _____
7. _____
8. _____

1 You should put it down.

Grammar and vocabulary | Complete the sentences with the phrasal verbs in the box. Add the correct pronouns.

look up	put away	put on	take apart	throw away
print out	✓ put down	set up	take off	turn off

1. Thanks for bringing in the box of groceries. Could you _put it down_ over here?
2. I did something awful to my computer. I tried to _____ , and now I can't get all the pieces back in it.
3. I hate those sticky price labels on things you buy. I can never _____ .
4. My game controller doesn't work anymore. I wonder if I should just _____ .
5. There's nothing good on TV. Do you mind if I _____ ?
6. I just bought these new headphones. Do you want to _____ and try them out?
7. I downloaded a video-chat app, but I can't _____ .
8. I don't know what this word means. Maybe I should _____ on the Internet.
9. My brother leaves his video games all over the floor. He should _____ , or they'll get damaged.
10. After you write documents, do you _____ to read them?

2 Step-by-step

Grammar and vocabulary | Complete the conversation with the words in the box.

hook up / the computer	✓ turn down / the air conditioning
pick up / the monitor	turn on / the radio
plug in / all the cables	turn up / the volume

Ruth We found this great apartment, but it's so cold in here.

Kate Oh, I'll _turn down the air conditioning_ .
There we go. So, what do you want to do first?

Ruth Let's put some music on.
Can you _____ ?

Kate Sure. Is that loud enough?

Ruth Not really. Can you _____ ? Thanks.

Kate I'd like to _____ , so I can check my email.

Ruth OK, let's put the computer over by the window.
I'll _____ .
You get the computer and the cables.

Kate OK. You know, I have no idea where to _____ .

Ruth I'm sure we can figure it out. Do you know where the manual is?

3 ▸ What to do?

Grammar and vocabulary | **Complete the conversations using the given words. Write A's suggestions in two different ways. Then use the correct pronoun in B's response.**

1. A Before you go out, _put on your hat and gloves_ .
   Before you go out, _put your hat and gloves on_ .
   (put on / your hat and gloves)

   B If I get too warm, can I _take them off_ ?
   (take off)

2. A _____ in a dictionary.
   _____ in a dictionary.
   (look up / the new words)

   B Can we _____ on the Internet?
   (look up)

3. A You have to _____ gently.
   You have to _____ gently.
   (put in / the DVD)

   B If it doesn't work, should I _____ ?
   (take out)

4. A The kitchen's so messy. We should _____ .
   The kitchen's so messy. We should _____ .
   (put away / the dishes)

   B Actually, why don't we _____ ?
   (throw away)

4 ▸ About you

Grammar | **Complete the questions. Then fill in the survey with true answers.**

	Yes	No

1. Can you explain to someone _how to set up voice mail on a phone_ ?
   (how / set up voice mail on a phone) ☐ ☐

2. Do you have any idea _____ on your computer?
   (where / plug in the headphones) ☐ ☐

3. Could you tell someone _____ ?
   (how / use your TV remote) ☐ ☐

4. Do you know _____ on the Internet?
   (how / look up information) ☐ ☐

5. Do you have any idea _____ when your computer crashes?
   (what / do) ☐ ☐

6. Do you know _____ on your computer?
   (how / change the password) ☐ ☐

Don't you think . . . ?

Conversation strategies

A Match Cameron's opinions with her friends' responses.

1. I think kids watch too much TV. _f_

2. I think video games are totally boring and stupid. _____

3. I don't think people should drive big cars. _____

4. It's a shame no one writes letters anymore. I used to love getting them. _____

5. Kids need to spend less time on the computer. _____

6. I don't like shopping on the Internet. You can't see what you're buying. _____

a. I know what you mean, but with email, you can get in touch with people more often and faster.

b. I'm not so sure. Don't you think they can learn a lot online, too? I mean, there are some good educational websites.

c. Maybe. People with large families need to have big cars, though.

d. I don't know. I find it saves me time because I don't have to go to the store and wait in line.

e. I know what you mean, but there are so many different kinds of games. You could probably find something you liked.

f. That's true. On the other hand, kids need to relax sometimes, and we all have our favorite shows.

B Write your own responses to Cameron's opinions in part A. Use the expressions in the box if you disagree with her.

I know what you mean, but . . .	I don't know.
I'm not (so) sure. Don't you think . . . ?	✓ That's true. . . . , though.
Maybe.	On the other hand, . . .

1. _That's true. I think some TV shows are educational, though._

2. _____
   _____

3. _____
   _____

4. _____
   _____

5. _____
   _____

6. _____
   _____

2 What's your opinion?

Conversation
strategies Write opinions about the topics. Then add an expression from the box to get someone
to agree with you. Use each expression twice.

> You know what I mean?   You know?   You know what I'm saying?

1. Texting is _really convenient. But it's really annoying when you're trying to have a_
   conversation with someone who's texting at the same time. You know what I mean?

2. Video calling is _____
   _____

3. Blogging is _____
   _____

4. Online video clips are _____
   _____

5. Tablets are _____
   _____

6. Social networking is _____
   _____

3 I don't know.

Conversation
strategies Respond to each statement with a different opinion. Try to convince the other person
to agree with you.

1. Kids spend too much time on the Internet.

   I don't know. I think it's great they learn how to use computers
   when they're so young. You know?

2. Teens shouldn't go to school and work at the same time. It's too hard.

   _____
   _____

3. I think too many people are addicted to their computers and phones and everything.

   _____
   _____

4. You never know if things you see on the Internet are true.

   _____
   _____

1 Spam-a-lot

Reading | **A** Read the article. Then check (✓) the best title.

☐ How to Be a Successful Spammer   ☐ How Companies Avoid Spam
☐ Where to Send Spam   ☐ Don't Be a Victim – How You Can Avoid Spam

Are you fed up with junk email and spam that fills up your inbox every day? Spam isn't just annoying for home users of computers. It's becoming a serious problem for businesses, too. Getting rid of spam wastes employees' time. Spam takes up space on computers, and it can slow down – or even jam – normal email traffic.

Most people don't know how spammers get their email address, but in fact, it's very easy. Your email address may be on any number of Internet sites such as blogs, email newsletters, company directories, and many other lists on the Web. You can also become a spam victim if you've entered an online contest or responded to a survey using your email address.

Spammers also use software that generates email addresses automatically. This software makes up millions of email addresses by using common names and the addresses of well-known companies and Internet service providers. It then sends out messages to all the addresses it creates. Although some of them might not work and the messages "bounce back," many others will get through to real people. The spammers now have a valuable list of valid addresses, which they can sell to other spammers at high prices.

HOW TO PROTECT YOURSELF FROM SPAM

DO:

▶ Change your email address regularly. Create an address that is difficult to guess. For example, if your name is Kevin Smith and you love cycling, try an address like KSmith4biking@cup.org. Or if you live in Toronto, you could use KS_in_Toronto@cup.org.

▶ Have two email addresses – one for public use and a private one only for friends and family.

▶ Buy anti-spam software or use email filters. Many email programs have filters that automatically send spam to a junk-mail folder. Be sure to check the junk-mail folder periodically for any personal mail that goes there by mistake.

▶ Pay attention to typos and misspellings in email subject lines. These are warning signs of possible spam.

DON'T:

▶ Respond to spam – ever. When you respond, you confirm that your address is valid.

▶ Buy anything from a company that sent you spam. This supports their belief that spamming makes money.

B Find the underlined words in the article. Then circle the best meaning.

1. Spam can <u>jam</u> normal email traffic.   a. slow down   ⓑ stop or block
2. You can become a <u>spam victim</u>.   a. someone who gets spam   b. someone who sends spam
3. The software <u>generates</u> addresses.   a. creates   b. gets rid of
4. Some messages "<u>bounce back</u>."   a. get to the people   b. go back to the spammers
5. They have a list of <u>valid</u> addresses.   a. real   b. false
6. Never <u>confirm</u> your address.   a. forget   b. say it's correct

2 Get rid of it!

Writing **A Read the list of ideas, and add an idea of your own. Then use the ideas to complete the article.**

Ways to prevent spam

- Get another email address. Use one email address for chat rooms and message boards.
- Tell friends and family how to prevent spam.
- Use spam-filtering software.
- Don't respond to spam.
- _____
  _____
  _____

How to get rid of spam

First of all, keep your personal email address private. If you want to participate in chat rooms or on _message boards_ , get a second _____ from a free email provider. Second, don't _____ to spam, even when it provides a link to "unsubscribe" from the list. Spammers see that your address is valid and sell it to other spammers. Third, use the _____ on your computer. Fourth, _____ .

Finally, tell _____ about these tips. If fewer people respond to spam, there will be less spam!

B Brainstorm ideas on one of these topics. Then plan and write a short article.

- How to avoid identity theft
- How to protect yourself from theft
- How to use the Internet safely
- How to get help with computer problems

Ideas

Unit 9 Progress chart

What can you do? Mark the boxes. ☑ = I can . . . ? = I need to review how to . . .	To review, go back to these pages in the Student's Book.
Grammar use questions within questions and statements.	86 and 87
use *how to*, *where to*, and *what to* + verb.	88
use separable phrasal verbs like *turn on* and *plug in*.	88
Vocabulary use at least 12 phrasal verbs.	88 and 89
Conversation strategies use expressions to give a different opinion.	90
use expressions to get someone to agree with me.	91
Writing brainstorm and organize ideas to plan an article.	93

73

What's up?

Lesson A / Catching up

1 What have they been doing?

Grammar | **A** What have these people been doing? What have they done? Complete the sentences using the present perfect continuous and then the present perfect.

1. Kazuo *'s been doing yard work* (do yard work). He *'s planted* (plant) some flowers.

2. Sienna and Lynn _____ (shop). They _____ (spend) over $500 each!

3. Lola _____ (run). She _____ just _____ (finish) a marathon.

4. Carmen _____ (cook) dinner. She _____ (grill) some fish.

5. Sal and Elena _____ (ski). They _____ (have) one lesson.

6. Tony _____ (do) laundry all morning. He _____ (wash) three loads.

B Circle the correct word to complete each sentence.

1. Kazuo's been doing yard work **since** /**for** a few hours.

2. Sienna and Lynn haven't shopped online **since** / **in** months.

3. Lola's been running **since** / **for** she was in college.

4. Carmen hasn't made unhealthy food **since** / **in** a long time.

5. Sal and Elena have been skiing **since** / **for** this morning.

6. Tony's been doing the laundry **for** / **in** over two hours.

2 Questions, questions . . .

Grammar | Read each situation. Then use the words to write questions and answers in the present perfect continuous or the present perfect.

1. You have a friend who has been taking Spanish lessons. You ask:

   A (how long / study / Spanish) *How long have you been studying Spanish?*

   B (seven months) *I've been studying Spanish for seven months.*

   A (how many words / learn) _____

   B (about 250) _____

2. You meet a famous baseball player. You ask:

   A (how long / play / baseball) _____

   B (18 years) _____

   A (how many games / win this season) _____

   B (12 out of 15) _____

3 About you

Grammar | **A** Complete the questions. Use the present perfect continuous or the present perfect.

1. What ____*have*____ you _*been doing*____ (do) lately after class?

2. How many times _____ you _____ (go) to the movies this month?

3. Who _____ you _____ (hang out) with recently?

4. How many times _____ you _____ (eat out) at a restaurant this week?

5. _____ you _____ (study) a lot lately?

6. How many phone calls _____ you _____ (make) this week?

7. How many times _____ you _____ (oversleep) in the last month?

8. What _____ you _____ (think) about for the last hour?

9. How many books _____ you _____ (read) this year?

10. _____ you _____ (exercise) lately?

B Answer the questions in part A with true information.

1. *I've been taking guitar lessons.*

2. _____

3. _____

4. _____

5. _____

6. _____

7. _____

8. _____

9. _____

10. _____

1 Crossword puzzle

Vocabulary | Complete the crossword puzzle.

Across

2. A movie with an exciting story and lots of suspense is a ___thriller___ .

3. A _____ movie is about soldiers.

5. In a romantic _____ , two people fall in love and funny things happen.

7. A movie about a real event is called a _____ story.

9. A movie that makes you cry is called a tear_____ .

10. An _____ movie has a fast-moving story and is often violent.

Down

1. A _____ -fiction movie often takes place in the future.

4. A movie with cartoon characters is an _____ movie.

6. A movie that has singing and dancing is a _____ .

8. _____ movies are often scary and have monsters in them.

2 Best of Bollywood

Vocabulary | Complete Daria's blog with the words in the box.

✓comedies	endings	love story	set in	subtitled
costumes	hilarious	play	stunts	take place

Daria's Blog □ ◻ ✕

Daria 12:31 p.m.
Some of my favorite movies are musicals from Bollywood, especially the romantic _comedies_ . The movies are usually _____ _____ India, and the actors often _____ characters who fall in love. I really enjoy a good _____ _____ . They can sometimes be tearjerkers, but the nice thing about Bollywood movies is that they often have happy _____ , so you leave the movie theater feeling good. Some of them are also very funny – the last one I saw was just _____ . Some of them are historical and _____ _____ in the past. These are my favorites because the colors and the _____ are wonderful. The movies aren't usually in English, but they're _____ , so you can read while you're watching. Sometimes the movies even have fight scenes with lots of special effects and _____ . They're really great!

3 About you

Vocabulary | Write reviews of movies you've seen. Complete each sentence with the title of a movie. Then write more about each one by answering the questions.

CHOOSE A MOVIE	What type of movie is it? What's it about? Who's in it? Did you like it? Why? Why not?
1. I really enjoyed _____ _____ *Les Misérables* _____ .	*It's a musical, and it's set in France in the 1800s. Hugh Jackman plays a man who escapes from prison. Russell Crowe is the police officer who chases him. I really enjoyed the movie. It has wonderful music, and the costumes are amazing.*
2. _____ _____ is playing right now.	
3. The best movie I've ever seen is _____ _____ .	
4. I didn't like _____ _____ .	

4 I still haven't see it.

Grammar and vocabulary | Complete the conversation with *already*, *still*, or *yet*.

Ann There are so many movies that I ____*still*____ haven't seen. Do you want to go see one tonight?

Gus Yeah, OK. Let's see. How about Brad Pitt's new movie? I haven't seen that _____.

Ann Oh, I've _____ seen that one. It was good. How about the new horror movie that's out? Have you seen that _____ ?

Gus No, I don't like scary movies. I'm 25, and I _____ haven't seen a horror movie.

Ann Well, there's a new animated movie out. I haven't seen that one _____ , either.

Gus Oh, great. Let's go. I've been dying to see it!

1 Favors

Conversation strategies | **Complete the conversations with the expressions in the box.**

I wanted to	I was wondering,
✓ I was wondering if I could	Would it be all right if I
I was wondering if you could	Would it be OK

1. **Victor** Hi, Raoul. What can I do for you?

   Raoul _I was wondering if I could_ talk to
   you for a moment. Is now OK?

   Victor No problem. Come on in.

   Raoul Thanks. _____
   worked from home tomorrow?

   Victor Tomorrow?

   Raoul Yes. Someone is coming to fix my stove,
   and I need to be home to let him in.
   _____ with you?

   Victor Yeah, sure. I don't see why not.

   Raoul Thanks, Victor. I really appreciate it.

2. **Dad** Hi, Josie. What's up?

   Josie Hey, Dad. _____
   ask you a favor.

   Dad Sure, what is it?

   Josie Well, _____ lend
   me some money – if that's OK.

   Dad Hmm. It depends. How much? And for
   what?

   Josie Well, I was thinking, your birthday is
   next week, right?

   Dad Yes, it is.

   Josie So, _____ could
   I borrow $50 to buy you your present?

2 Can I borrow the car?

Conversation strategies Stephanie's friend Ally is coming for a visit. Stephanie needs to ask her roommate Jenny for some favors. Look at her list, and complete each of her requests.

> *Things I need to do:*
> 1. Ask Jenny if Ally can stay here.
> 2. Pick up Ally at airport – borrow Jenny's car.
> 3. See if Jenny wants to go sightseeing with us Saturday.
> 4. Organize a party Saturday night – check with Jenny.
> 5. Check Ally's return flight online – use Jenny's computer.

1. I wanted to *ask you if Ally could stay here* .

2. I was wondering if I could _____ .

3. I was wondering, _____ ?

4. Would it be all right _____ ?

5. Would it be OK with you if I _____ ?

3 All right. What time?

Conversation strategies Choose the best sentence to continue each conversation. Then write *A* if the speaker is agreeing, *M* if the speaker is moving the conversation along, or *U* to show the speaker understands.

1. A I'm going grocery shopping later, and I was wondering if you could come and help me. [A]
   B ☑ All right. What time?
      ☐ That's OK.

2. A Do you have time to talk now? [ ]
   B Sure. Let me just put these papers away.
      ☐ Um, OK, I guess so.
      ☐ All right. What did you want to talk about?

3. A This pasta is delicious! Could you give me the recipe? [ ]
   B ☐ Sure. It's very easy.
      ☐ That would be OK.

4. A Can you help me with something? [ ]
   B ☐ OK. What do you need?
      ☐ That's all right.

5. A I'm leaving early today. [ ]
   B ☐ Right. I remember you have an appointment.
      ☐ OK. I think so, too.

1 Weekend favorites

Reading | **A** Read the reviews. What things are reviewed? Check (✓) the boxes.

☐ a book ☐ a movie ☐ a phone app ☐ a video game ☐ a Web app

Weekend Blog ⬜ ⬜ ✕

THINGS TO KEEP YOU BUSY ON WEEKENDS

1. MOVIE EFFECTIVE

With Movie Effective, you can add special effects to your videos. Simply record a video with your smartphone camera. Then add exciting effects — just like they do in the movies. The app comes with two effects — lightning and slow motion — but you can also buy others, like sound effects. Even though I don't usually shoot or share videos personally, I found this to be a lot of fun. So, be careful — it's addictive, and you may get totally hooked!

2. ACCUSED

I really enjoyed playing this game. It combines a science-fiction setting with great action. You are a character who is wrongly accused of a crime. You have to find out who the real criminal is and get justice. Your choices determine the storyline. The action is fast-moving and there are some sad moments, so if you're very sensitive, this may not be the video game for you. However, the amazing setting and the ability to create your own story make this a great game for most players.

3. RECORDYOURRUN

If you are serious about running, hiking, biking, or even skiing, and have been wondering how to keep track of your progress, this phone app is the answer. It records your pace, distance, and time, and you can save your results and compare different exercise sessions. You can set goals for each time you go out and share your progress with friends. There's also a feature that lets your friends and family follow your progress in a race on a map. This app is the perfect way to mix technology and exercise.

4. FRETENDS

FretEnds has a fabulous Web app that will teach you how to play the guitar. You can choose to play a real guitar or a virtual one. There are eight levels of play. If you start at the beginner level, you will learn to play "Brown Eyed Girl." You need to let the app access the microphone on your computer, so it can "hear" you play. Each song is broken down into small parts. After you've learned one part, you can move on. This app is great for everyone, whether you've never played or even if you've been playing for years.

B Read the article again. Write *T* (true) or *F* (false) for each sentence. Then correct the false sentences.

1. Movie Effective helps you record videos on your smartphone. __*F*__

2. The special effects on Movie Effective are all free. _____

3. *Accused* is a romantic comedy. _____

4. *Accused* is suitable for everyone. _____

5. RecordYourRun is for people who take exercise seriously. _____

6. With RecordYourRun, people can see if their friends are winning a race. _____

7. You need to buy a guitar before you can use the FretEnds app. _____

8. The FretEnds app is not for experienced players. _____

2 Music review

Writing **A** Read the music review. Complete the sentences with *although*, *even though*, or *even if* to contrast ideas. Sometimes more than one answer is possible.

_____ *Come Away With Me* was amazingly successful and really introduced Norah Jones to the world, *Little Broken Hearts* is a much better album. Most of her earlier work uses a lot of piano, but this album focuses more on the guitar, so the sound is different. _____ most of these songs are about heartbreak, the music is beautiful and sweet. _____ you don't like sad romantic songs, you will find something to enjoy in this new collection.

– *Music Scene* magazine

B Write a review of a movie, an album, or a TV show. Use *although*, *even though*, and *even if* to contrast ideas.

Unit 10 Progress chart

What can you do? Mark the boxes. ✔ = I can . . . ? = I need to review how to . . .	To review, go back to these pages in the Student's Book.
Grammar	
use the present perfect and present perfect continuous.	98 and 99
use *since*, *for*, and *in* with the present perfect to show duration.	99
use *already*, *still*, and *yet* with the present perfect.	101
Vocabulary	
name at least 6 different kinds of movies.	100 and 101
talk about movies using at least 15 new words and expressions.	100 and 101
Conversation strategies	
ask for a favor politely.	102
use *All right*, *OK*, and *Sure* to agree to requests; *All right*, *OK*, and *So* to move a conversation to a new phase or topic; and *Right* to show I agree or understand.	103
Writing	
use *although*, *even though*, and *even if* to contrast ideas.	105

Impressions

Lesson A / Speculating

1 It could be . . .

Grammar | Complete the sentences with the expressions in the box. Then write a second sentence using the cues and an appropriate modal.

| can't be the winners | may be taking a driving test | ✓ must be learning to drive |
| could be taking a hard test | might be the best student | must be the winners |

1. He _must be learning to drive_ .
   It could / might / may be his first lesson.
   (It / be / his first lesson)

2. He _____ .
   _____
   (It / be / his first lesson)

3. She _____ .
   _____
   (She / feel proud)

4. She _____ .
   _____
   (She / be nervous)

5. They _____ .
   _____
   (They / practice a lot)

6. They _____ .
   _____
   (They / be disappointed)

2 He must be crazy!

Grammar Circle the correct words to complete the sentences.

1. Mandy   What's he doing? He (**must be**) / **can't be** crazy!

   Molly   He **might be** / **can't be** an acrobat with the circus.

   Mandy   You're right. He **must practice** / **must be practicing**
   for tonight's show.

   Molly   That's amazing! I mean, it **can't be** / **might be** easy
   to bend like that.

   Mandy   Yeah, it **could be** / **must not be** painful, too.

   Molly   Well, I certainly won't try that!

2. Jason   How old is that kid? She **must be** / **can't be** more
   than five years old.

   Peter   Yeah, you're right. She **must not be** / **might be** about
   four or five.

   Jason   She's really good. She **must play** / **must be playing**
   every day for hours and hours.

   Peter   She makes it look so easy, too. I wonder what her
   parents think. They **could be** / **must be** so proud.

   Jason   Yeah, she **could be** / **can't be** the youngest
   professional piano player in the world.

3 About you

Grammar Think of someone you know who is not in the room with you now. Answer the
questions about him or her using *must, may, might, could,* or *can't.*

1. Where do you think he or she is right now?

   It's Saturday afternoon, so he might be on the golf course. He can't be at work.

2. What do you think he or she is doing?

   _____

3. How do you think he or she is feeling?

   _____

4. What do you think he or she is wearing?

   _____

5. Who do you think he or she is with?

   _____

6. What do you think he or she is thinking about right now?

   _____

1 Scrambled up

Grammar and vocabulary

A Write the adjective for each definition. You can check your answers in a dictionary. Then use the letters in the boxes to answer the question below.

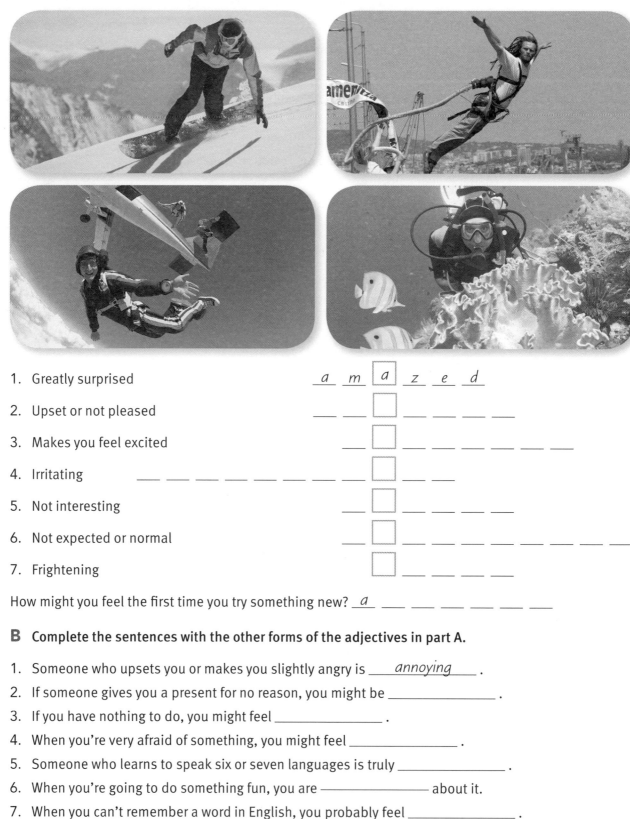

1. Greatly surprised   _a_ _m_ [_a_] _z_ _e_ _d_

2. Upset or not pleased   __ __ [ ] __ __ __ __ __

3. Makes you feel excited   __ [ ] __ __ __ __ __ __

4. Irritating   __ __ __ __ __ __ __ __ [ ] __ __

5. Not interesting   __ [ ] __ __ __ __ __

6. Not expected or normal   __ [ ] __ __ __ __ __ __ __ __

7. Frightening   [ ] __ __ __ __

How might you feel the first time you try something new? _a_ __ __ __ __ __ __

B Complete the sentences with the other forms of the adjectives in part A.

1. Someone who upsets you or makes you slightly angry is _____annoying_____ .

2. If someone gives you a present for no reason, you might be _____ .

3. If you have nothing to do, you might feel _____ .

4. When you're very afraid of something, you might feel _____ .

5. Someone who learns to speak six or seven languages is truly _____ .

6. When you're going to do something fun, you are —————————— about it.

7. When you can't remember a word in English, you probably feel _____ .

2 Good news, bad news

Complete the emails. Use the correct forms of the adjectives.

New Message — □ ×

To: EmmaP@cup.com
From: shak91@cup.com
Subject: **My short story**

Hey Emma,

I'm so ___excited___ (excite). Remember the short story I wrote for English class last month? Well, my teacher sent it to a competition, and guess what? It won first prize! The judges said my story was very _____ (interest). I knew my teacher was _____ (please) with my work. She said my story was _____ (fascinate). But I never thought she would enter it in a competition! I was totally _____ (shock) when she told me. And all my classmates were totally _____ (jealous). What's new and exciting with you?

Shakira

New Message — □ ×

To: shak91@cup.com
From: EmmaP@cup.com
Subject: **My short story**

Hi Shakira,

Congratulations! I wish I had _____ (excite) news for you, too, but I don't. Unfortunately, I failed my driver's test last week. I was really _____ (disappoint). It's just so _____ (embarrass) – it's the third time I've failed the test. The driving instructor told me to make a right-hand turn, and I turned left instead. I guess I got a little _____ (confuse). I could tell the instructor was really _____ (annoy) with me! My dad told me not to get _____ (frustrate). He said he failed his driver's test five times before he finally passed, but I'm starting to get _____ (worry). Well, talk to you later.

Emma

---

3 About you

How would you feel in these situations? Complete the sentences with true information.

1. You fail a test that you have studied very hard for.

   I would feel _disappointed if I failed a test that I thought I was prepared for_ .

   It might be _embarrassing if my friends found out_ .

2. Your friend doesn't show up for a date.

   I would get _____ .

   I might feel _____ .

3. You are home alone during a storm.

   I might feel _____ .

   It could be _____ .

4. Someone is telling you a story you've already heard ten times.

   I might feel _____ .

   I would probably think _____ .

Lesson C / That must be fun.

1 You must be excited.

Conversation strategies Complete the responses in the conversations to show understanding. Use *must be* and an adjective.

1. I'm learning how to design a website.   *That must be hard* _____ .

2. My brother always takes my stuff.   That _____ .

3. I lost my wallet and credit cards at the mall.   You _____ .

4. I'm going to climb Mount Rainier next month.   You _____ .

5. I didn't win the poetry contest.   You _____ .

6. My ex-boyfriend is dating my best friend.   That _____ .

2 Explanations

Conversation strategies Complete the conversation with *you see* or *I see*, or leave a blank where neither one is appropriate.

Walt Hi, Reg. I'm sorry I'm late. I didn't hear my alarm.
_You see_____ , I was working on my report until about 3:30 this morning.

Reg Uh-huh, _____ . So, will it be ready for the meeting with the boss?

Walt _____ Yes. I just have to make some copies. What time is the meeting?

Reg Well, it was at 11:00, but the boss called me about half an hour ago, and it's now at 2:30. She's meeting someone for lunch, _____ , and she has to leave at 11:30.

Walt Oh, _____ . So, I guess I didn't have to rush.

Reg Well, at least it's all done now, and you can relax.

3 An author in Paris

Conversation strategies **Complete the conversation with the expressions in the box. Use each expression twice.**

I see	that must be	you must be	you see

Akina   Hey, Omar. I hear you're going away for a while. Where to?

Omar   Yeah, I'm leaving for Paris next week.

Akina   You're kidding! Wow, _you must be_ excited!

Omar   I am. I've never been there before. _____ , I'm going to do some research for my next book. That's always the best part – the research.

Akina   I bet. _____ fun. So, what's your book about?

Omar   It's a love story, of course.

Akina   _____ . Uh . . . can you share any details yet?

Omar   I guess. Hmm . . . let's see. It's about a young girl who goes to visit a friend in Paris. And well, you know, she meets a mysterious young man, they fall in love, and lots of things happen.

Akina   Really? What kind of things?

Omar   Well, I don't want to say yet. _____ , I want to keep the details a surprise.

Akina   I understand. But, gosh, _____ hard. I can never keep secrets.

Omar   I know what you mean. It's difficult sometimes.

Akina   So, tell me what else you're doing in Paris.

Omar   Oh. I'm going to read from my last novel at an English-language bookstore.

Akina   Great! _____ pleased about that. Will you be nervous?

Omar   No, not at all. I've done it several times. It's part of the job of being a writer.

Akina   _____ . Well, have a wonderful trip. Good luck with your research.

Omar   Thanks. I'll tell you all about it when I get back.

1 Child prodigies

Reading | **A** Read the article. What does "child prodigy" mean?

☐ someone under the age of 15   ☐ a child with a special talent   ☐ a child who is famous

CHILD PRODIGIES:

Nature OR Nurture?

Mozart wrote his first minuet at age six. Cellist Yo-Yo Ma first performed in public at the age of five. William James Sidis read Homer in Greek at age four and was the youngest person ever to attend Harvard University at 11. Ukrainian chess player Sergey Karjakin became the youngest international grand master at 12. Pablo Picasso first publicly exhibited his paintings at age 13.

Many parents may hope for a genius child, but there can be a price to pay. Some child prodigies never experience a normal childhood, often because it's difficult for them to make friends, and they suffer socially. Some genius children even have mental breakdowns at an early age, and gifted child athletes or musicians can be permanently injured from practicing too hard.

We often hear stories of parents who push their children too hard. However, some experts say that for the most part, "pushy parent" is an unfair label: Parents don't push prodigies, prodigies push parents. Many gifted children quickly become bored with school and homework that is too easy. For these kids, school is frustrating, and they risk losing interest in it altogether. It's better to allow these children to skip grades, experts say, than to let them become disappointed in school.

Are prodigies born, or are they created? The short answer is: we don't know. Certainly, many parents of gifted children provide a stimulating environment: They read to their children at an early age, take them to museums and concerts, and give them a lot of independence. But experts advise parents not to be disappointed if their child isn't an early genius. Mozart was a child prodigy; Einstein was not. But the world is still amazed by them both.

B Find a word or expression in the article for each meaning below.

1. go to, or be present at (a place or an event) (paragraph 1) ___attend___
2. psychological problems (paragraph 2) _____
3. talented; exceptional (paragraph 3) _____
4. interesting; encouraging you to learn (paragraph 4) _____

C Read the article again. Then answer the questions.

1. Who's the youngest prodigy mentioned in the article?

   _____

2. What are three disadvantages of being a child prodigy?

   _____

3. What problems do some gifted children have with school?

   _____

4. How do some parents help their gifted children develop?

   _____

2 My child is a prodigy!

Writing | **A** Read the letter from a parent to a school principal. Circle the expressions that give impressions or opinions. Underline the statements that are stated as fact.

MT

Dear Dr. Evans,

My child is enrolled in your school. (I believe that) he is a very gifted student, and I feel that he is bored in his classes. It seems to me that he is becoming increasingly frustrated and anxious because he has lost interest in school. Last year he was the top student in his class, but this year his grades are slipping. My impression is that he needs to take more difficult classes. In my opinion, he is not finding his current classes challenging enough. Can you help?

Sincerely,

Marsha Taylor

B Write a letter to the editor of a local newspaper about one of the topics below or your own idea. Use the expressions from part A.

- There aren't enough leisure facilities for local teens.
- We need healthier food options in schools.
- There's too much litter on city streets.

Unit 11 Progress chart

What can you do? Mark the boxes. ✓ = I can . . . ? = I need to review how to . . .	To review, go back to these pages in the Student's Book.
Grammar ☐ use the modals *must*, *may*, *might*, *can't*, and *could* to speculate.	108 and 109
☐ use adjectives ending in *-ed* to describe how someone feels.	110 and 111
☐ use adjectives ending in *-ing* to describe someone or something.	110 and 111
Vocabulary ☐ name at least 12 adjectives to describe feelings and reactions.	110 and 111
Conversation strategies ☐ use *That must be* or *You must be* + adjective to show I understand.	112
☐ use *You see* to explain something and *I see* to show I understand.	113
Writing ☐ use expressions like *I feel* to give impressions or opinions.	115

Lesson A / Local news

1 And now, the news . . .

Grammar | **Complete the news reports. Use the simple past passive.**

1. Newtown Park train station __*was closed*__
   (close) this morning after a bag _____
   (find) on a train. Several trains _____
   (delay), and some _____ (cancel). The
   bag _____ (remove) from the station
   and _____ (search). Police said later
   that the bag was full of clothes. The train station
   _____ (reopen) after two hours.

2. A woman _____ (rescue) earlier today
   after she climbed onto her roof to repair her
   chimney. Firefighters _____ (call) to the
   scene after neighbors heard the woman shout
   for help. Fortunately, the woman _____
   (not hurt), but she _____ (take) to the
   local hospital and _____ (release) later
   this afternoon.

3. The National Museum _____ (break into)
   last night, and three valuable paintings
   _____ (steal). The area around the
   museum _____ (close off) following the
   incident, and bystanders _____
   (interview). Police are now looking for two young
   men who _____ (see) nearby.

2 More news

Grammar | **Rewrite the sentences using the simple past passive.**

1. They delayed the game for two hours.   _The game was delayed for two hours._
2. Someone stole a ring from an exhibit.   _____
3. They canceled the rock concert.   _____
4. A woman found a wallet on a bus.   _____
5. They took two people to the hospital.   _____
6. Someone rescued a man from a fire.   _____

3 What happened?

Grammar | **Look at the picture. What do you think happened? Write a news report. Use the verbs in the box or your own ideas. Use the simple past passive. Be creative with your facts!**

break into

close

find

hurt

open

rob

steal

take

News Report: Stolen Goods!
A downtown jewelry store was robbed yesterday.

1 All kinds of weather

Vocabulary | **Look at the pictures. Complete the sentences with the words in the box.**

aftershocks	floods	hurricane	✓rains	tornado
earthquake	hailstorm	lightning	thunderstorm	winds

1. The region was hit by heavy ____*rains*____ earlier today. Several roads were closed because of flash _____ .

2. Farmers say their crops were badly damaged by the ice from a freak _____ that passed through the area today.

3. Parts of the country were damaged by a _____ yesterday.

4. Airports were closed today due to _____ Albert. Flights were canceled because of strong _____ and rain.

5. The area was hit yesterday by a major _____ , measuring 5.6 on the Richter scale. _____ were felt throughout the area.

6. Electricity throughout the city was disrupted by thunder and _____ from a severe _____ .

2 What was the cause?

Grammar and vocabulary | Look at each pair of pictures. What caused the damage? Write a sentence using the given word and *by*.

start

1. _A fire was started by a candle._

blow down

2. _____

strike

3. _____

cause

4. _____

crack

5. _____

3 In the news

Grammar | Rewrite the sentences using the simple past passive and the adverb given.

1. The fire damaged the building. (partially)
   The building was partially damaged by the fire.

2. The storm disrupted train services. (temporarily)

   _____

3. Flash floods damaged several houses in the area. (badly)

   _____

4. A wildfire injured three firefighters. (seriously)

   _____

5. A tornado destroyed a small farm. (completely)

   _____

1 News travels fast!

Conversation strategies | Complete the conversation with the expressions in the box. Use each expression only once.

| did I tell you | guess what | you know |
| did you hear about | ✓have you heard | you know what |

Don   _Have you heard_ the news about Henry?

Nadia   No. What happened to him?

Don   Well, _____ he goes mountain biking, right?

Nadia   Yes. I've seen him on his bike a lot.

Don   Well, he went out biking yesterday, and _____ ? He was in the mountains during that big thunderstorm in the afternoon. He had to sit under a tree to avoid the lightning. . . .

Nadia   Under a tree? _____ ? That's really dangerous.

Don   It is?

Nadia   Oh, yeah. _____ those golfers who were hit by lightning under a tree?

Don   No. Oh, that's awful.

Nadia   Yeah. They were taken to the hospital and everything. But amazingly, they were OK.

Don   That was lucky. By the way, _____ about my car? The roof was damaged in that storm, too. It was hit by the hailstones.

2 About you

Conversation strategies | Write sentences introducing some news. Use true information.

1. _You know my friend Callie? She got a new laptop for her birthday._
   (good news about a friend)

2. _____
   (fun news about yourself)

3. _____
   (bad news about a local sports team)

4. _____
   (news about the local weather)

5. _____
   (interesting news about your favorite actor or singer)

6. _____
   (news about a family member)

7. _____
   (news about another city)

3 The funny thing was . . .

Conversation strategies | **Circle the best way to complete each sentence.**

1. I lost my bag last week, and then I found it outside my dorm room. The funny thing was, **everything was stolen** /(**nothing was stolen**).

2. Thieves broke into my car last week, and the worst thing was, **they took my favorite bag** / **the inside of the car was completely cleaned**.

3. Some neighbors of ours got married last month, and the weird thing is, **they didn't tell anyone about it** / **we all had a great time**.

4. We had a great weekend at the beach. The best thing was, **the water was so warm** / **it rained**.

5. That movie was incredible. The only thing was, **the ending was the best** / **the ending was disappointing**.

6. We went out for dinner last night, and the food was terrible. The other thing was, **the waiters were helpful** / **it was really expensive**.

4 The whole story

Conversation strategies | **Complete the conversations with the expressions in the box.**

Did I tell you?	The best thing is,
✓ Did you hear	The funny thing is,

1. A _Did you hear_____ about the new vacation schedule?

   B No, I didn't. What about it?

   A We get an extra week of vacation.

   B Great!

   A _____ the extra week is in February. That means we can plan a nice, long ski vacation!

2. A _____ There was a small fire at school yesterday.

   B Really? Where?

   A It was in the science lab. Some students were doing an experiment, and it exploded.

   B I hope no one was hurt.

   A Everyone is fine. _____ the students all got A's!

Lesson D / Reporting the news

1 Only the news that interests you

Reading | **A** Read the article. Which news sources do young people use?

CHANGING SOURCES OF NEWS

Far fewer people, especially the young, get their news from traditional news sources (either print or television), according to the most recent surveys. Instead, they are getting news from online sources and social networking sites, using their cell phones, tablets, and other mobile devices. In just two years, the number of people who get news from social networks doubled, and now about a third of young readers get their news this way. Although half of all Americans still watch TV to keep up with events, only 28% of people between the ages of 18 and 29 do so.

This use of social networks for news can be seen in Europe also. One in five people in the United Kingdom, and 43% of young people, get their news from the most popular social networking and microblogging sites. According to a recent study in Spain, three-quarters of the people between the ages of 16 and 30 got their news from a social networking site, as compared to only 28% from newspapers.

The addition of these news channels may contribute to "news fatigue," or a feeling of being overloaded with news. A study that was conducted by the University of Texas found that the way we get the news affects whether we feel information overload. People who got their news from computers and tablets were much more likely to feel overloaded, while people who got their news from TV or read it on their cell phone were less likely to experience this. The study showed that reading the same news on a computer was felt to be more tiring than reading it on a phone, perhaps because options seem more limited on a phone, and so more manageable. People on computers and tablets usually see many more links than people who use phone apps.

News organizations have adapted their news presentation style to try to prevent or reduce news fatigue. Some provide news in three forms: breaking headlines, short present-tense stories, and links to longer stories. By cutting down the number of headline updates, they also hope to reduce news fatigue.

B Read the article again. Circle the best alternatives to complete the sentences.

1. The author suggests in the article that young people and older people _____ .
   a. get news the same way   (b.) often get their news from different sources

2. One news source that is growing in popularity is _____ .
   a. microblogging sites   b. television news

3. Three out of four young people get their news from social networks in _____ .
   a. Spain   b. the United States

4. People who get their news on computers are more likely to be overloaded than if they get their news on _____ .
   a. tablets   b. smartphones

5. One way that people get news fatigue is by reading too many _____ .
   a. headline updates   b. longer stories

96

2 News survey

Writing **A Read the survey. Then complete the article below with the expressions in the box.**

Barnesville News Survey:

1. Do you read the *Barnesville News* every day?   👍**Yes** 49%   👎**No** 51%

2. What's your favorite section?

Section		%
Weather		0%
Local	▬	9%
Sports	▬	10%
Arts	▬▬	20%
International	▬▬▬▬▬	59%
Travel	▮	2%

almost
✓half
majority
none
out of
20%

About ___half___ of the people we surveyed read the *Barnesville News* every day. The _____ of *Barnesville News* readers prefer the international section. Only one _____ ten readers chose the sports section as their favorite. _____ 10% of readers enjoy the local section, while _____ of them are interested in the arts section. _____ of them chose the weather as their favorite.

B How many of your friends read a local or national news website?
Write a paragraph like the one in part A to show the statistics.

Unit 12 Progress chart

What can you do? Mark the boxes. ✓ = I can . . . ? = I need to review how to . . .	To review, go back to these pages in the Student's Book.
Grammar	
☐ use the simple past passive to discuss the news.	118, 119, and 120
☐ use the passive + *by* to introduce the "doer" or cause of an action.	120 and 121
Vocabulary	
☐ name at least 10 types of extreme weather or natural disasters.	120 and 121
☐ name at least 4 adverbs with the simple past passive.	120 and 121
Conversation strategies	
☐ introduce news with expressions like *Guess what?*	122
☐ use expressions like *The thing is . . .* to introduce issues.	123
Writing	
☐ write about statistics.	125

Illustration credits

Photo credits

Text credits

The top 500 spoken words

This is a list of the top 500 words in spoken North American English. It is based on a sample of four and a half million words of conversation from the Cambridge International Corpus. The most frequent word, *I*, is at the top of the list.

1. I	40. really	79. see
2. and	41. with	80. how
3. the	42. he	81. they're
4. you	43. one	82. kind
5. uh	44. are	83. here
6. to	45. this	84. from
7. a	46. there	85. did
8. that	47. I'm	86. something
9. it	48. all	87. too
10. of	49. if	88. more
11. yeah	50. no	89. very
12. know	51. get	90. want
13. in	52. about	91. little
14. like	53. at	92. been
15. they	54. out	93. things
16. have	55. had	94. an
17. so	56. then	95. you're
18. was	57. because	96. said
19. but	58. go	97. there's
20. is	59. up	98. I've
21. it's	60. she	99. much
22. we	61. when	100. where
23. huh	62. them	101. two
24. just	63. can	102. thing
25. oh	64. would	103. her
26. do	65. as	104. didn't
27. don't	66. me	105. other
28. that's	67. mean	106. say
29. well	68. some	107. back
30. for	69. good	108. could
31. what	70. got	109. their
32. on	71. OK	110. our
33. think	72. people	111. guess
34. right	73. now	112. yes
35. not	74. going	113. way
36. um	75. were	114. has
37. or	76. lot	115. down
38. my	77. your	116. we're
39. be	78. time	117. any

The top 500 spoken words

118. he's	161. five	204. sort
119. work	162. always	205. great
120. take	163. school	206. bad
121. even	164. look	207. we've
122. those	165. still	208. another
123. over	166. around	209. car
124. probably	167. anything	210. true
125. him	168. kids	211. whole
126. who	169. first	212. whatever
127. put	170. does	213. twenty
128. years	171. need	214. after
129. sure	172. us	215. ever
130. can't	173. should	216. find
131. pretty	174. talking	217. care
132. gonna	175. last	218. better
133. stuff	176. thought	219. hard
134. come	177. doesn't	220. haven't
135. these	178. different	221. trying
136. by	179. money	222. give
137. into	180. long	223. I'd
138. went	181. used	224. problem
139. make	182. getting	225. else
140. than	183. same	226. remember
141. year	184. four	227. might
142. three	185. every	228. again
143. which	186. new	229. pay
144. home	187. everything	230. try
145. will	188. many	231. place
146. nice	189. before	232. part
147. never	190. though	233. let
148. only	191. most	234. keep
149. his	192. tell	235. children
150. doing	193. being	236. anyway
151. cause	194. bit	237. came
152. off	195. house	238. six
153. I'll	196. also	239. family
154. maybe	197. use	240. wasn't
155. real	198. through	241. talk
156. why	199. feel	242. made
157. big	200. course	243. hundred
158. actually	201. what's	244. night
159. she's	202. old	245. call
160. day	203. done	246. saying

The top 500 spoken words

247. dollars	290. started	333. believe
248. live	291. job	334. thinking
249. away	292. says	335. funny
250. either	293. play	336. state
251. read	294. usually	337. until
252. having	295. wow	338. husband
253. far	296. exactly	339. idea
254. watch	297. took	340. name
255. week	298. few	341. seven
256. mhm	299. child	342. together
257. quite	300. thirty	343. each
258. enough	301. buy	344. hear
259. next	302. person	345. help
260. couple	303. working	346. nothing
261. own	304. half	347. parents
262. wouldn't	305. looking	348. room
263. ten	306. someone	349. today
264. interesting	307. coming	350. makes
265. am	308. eight	351. stay
266. sometimes	309. love	352. mom
267. bye	310. everybody	353. sounds
268. seems	311. able	354. change
269. heard	312. we'll	355. understand
270. goes	313. life	356. such
271. called	314. may	357. gone
272. point	315. both	358. system
273. ago	316. type	359. comes
274. while	317. end	360. thank
275. fact	318. least	361. show
276. once	319. told	362. thousand
277. seen	320. saw	363. left
278. wanted	321. college	364. friends
279. isn't	322. ones	365. class
280. start	323. almost	366. already
281. high	324. since	367. eat
282. somebody	325. days	368. small
283. let's	326. couldn't	369. boy
284. times	327. gets	370. paper
285. guy	328. guys	371. world
286. area	329. god	372. best
287. fun	330. country	373. water
288. they've	331. wait	374. myself
289. you've	332. yet	375. run

376. they'll	418. company	460. sorry
377. won't	419. friend	461. living
378. movie	420. set	462. drive
379. cool	421. minutes	463. outside
380. news	422. morning	464. bring
381. number	423. between	465. easy
382. man	424. music	466. stop
383. basically	425. close	467. percent
384. nine	426. leave	468. hand
385. enjoy	427. wife	469. gosh
386. bought	428. knew	470. top
387. whether	429. pick	471. cut
388. especially	430. important	472. computer
389. taking	431. ask	473. tried
390. sit	432. hour	474. gotten
391. book	433. deal	475. mind
392. fifty	434. mine	476. business
393. months	435. reason	477. anybody
394. women	436. credit	478. takes
395. month	437. dog	479. aren't
396. found	438. group	480. question
397. side	439. turn	481. rather
398. food	440. making	482. twelve
399. looks	441. American	483. phone
400. summer	442. weeks	484. program
401. hmm	443. certain	485. without
402. fine	444. less	486. moved
403. hey	445. must	487. gave
404. student	446. dad	488. yep
405. agree	447. during	489. case
406. mother	448. lived	490. looked
407. problems	449. forty	491. certainly
408. city	450. air	492. talked
409. second	451. government	493. beautiful
410. definitely	452. eighty	494. card
411. spend	453. wonderful	495. walk
412. happened	454. seem	496. married
413. hours	455. wrong	497. anymore
414. war	456. young	498. you'll
415. matter	457. places	499. middle
416. supposed	458. girl	500. tax
417. worked	459. happen	